Diving at the Moon
醉月而逝

Poetry by Kevin Gallagher

Diving at the Moon

And Yet it Moves

The Wild Goose

The Apprentice from Drogheda

Loom

Come Over and Help Us

Gringo Guadalupe

Looking for Lake Texcoco

Isolate Flecks

Ceremonial Entries:

The Poetry of Joseph DeRoche

(edited with Martha Collins)

spoKe

There's No Place on Earth Like the World:

compost's greatest hits

(edited with Margaret Bezucha)

DIVING AT THE MOON
醉月而逝

Poems by Kevin Gallagher
凯文.嘎拉格

Translated by Wang Ping
王屏译

SPUYTEN DUYVIL
New York City

ISBN 978-1-969900-12-9

Cover image: Wang Shimin (1592-1680), Album after Du Fu's Poems, The Palace Museum, Beijing China, Wikicommons.

"Tiantan Gongyuan" was previously published in the Harvard Review.

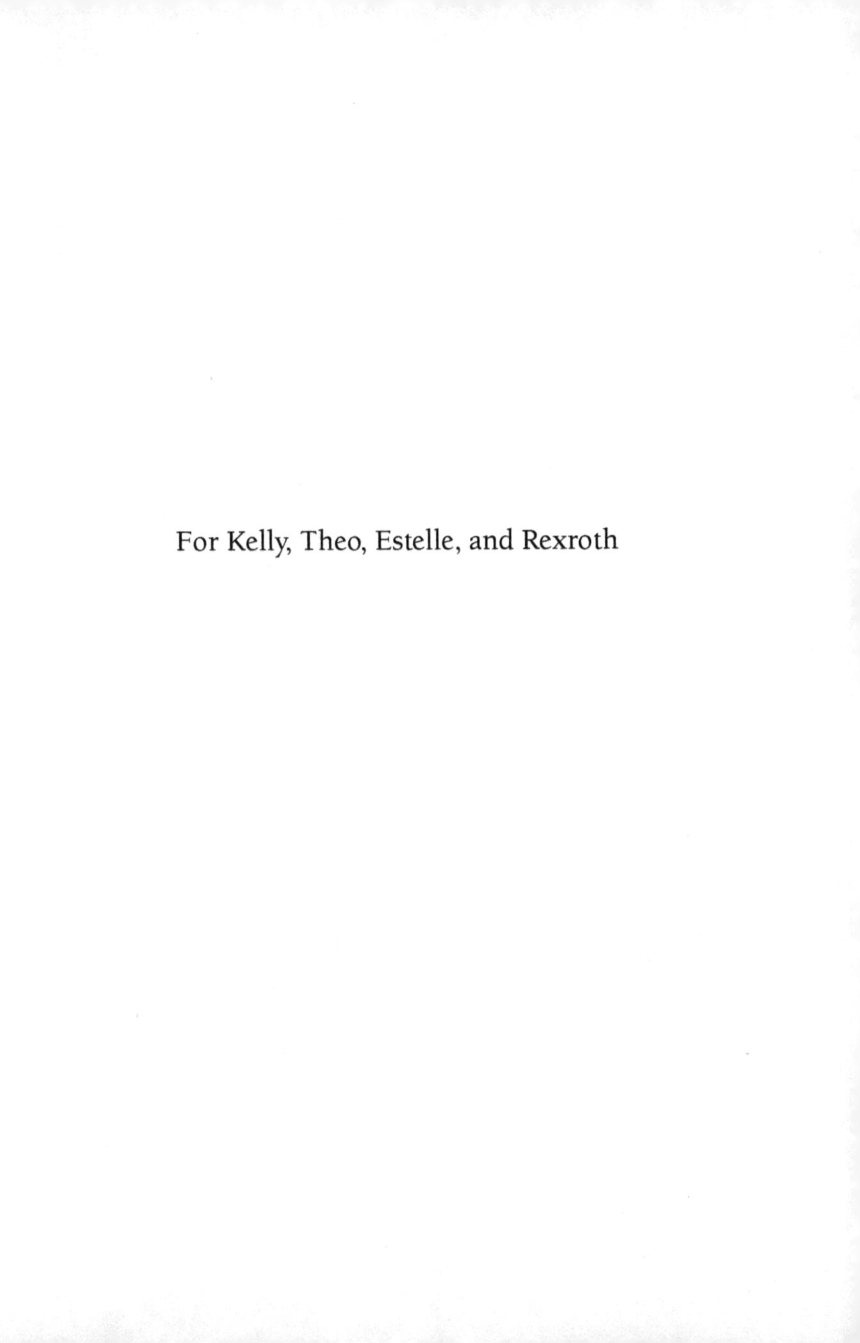

For Kelly, Theo, Estelle, and Rexroth

Contents

Regulated Archaeology
被监管的考古

Song of the Central Plain

Everything around us is so damn new.
I can't see where this escalator goes.

Wherever it goes it will never break.
It is hard to imagine the Mongols

stomping through this city in chariots
or the Yellow River flooding this place.

My skiff can't counter the tanker currents.
Beyond the haze the Qin Mountains still hold.

《中原之歌》

我们周围的一切太新了。
这电梯一眼望不到尽头。

而且不会破碎，无论到哪儿。
谁能想象当年的蒙古人

驾着战车碾过这座城市
或黄河在这里泛滥成灾。

我的小船如何抵挡货轮的尾流。
雾霭之外，秦岭依旧。

GUAUNYIN

The head's roundness resembles the heavens.
The feet's squareness resembles the earth.

The eyes and the ears are the sun and the moon.
The blood and spirit are the wind and rain.

One pitch-pipe or a lute string induces
an echo and embrace from the other.

An earthquake, eclipse, meteor, or flood
is a response to our performances.

《观音》

双足方正，插入地脉，
头颅浑圆，直冲苍穹。

日月为眸，普照春秋，
气化风雨，奔涌不休。

一管一弦，相呼相拥，
天地如琴，和鸣其中。

山崩星陨，潮汐蚀空，
不过人间，一缕颤动。

Winter Poems

I

The sky is celebrating the season
with swirling confetti of heavy snow.

I cannot see the mountains or the trees.
I can only hear the heavy winds below.

I can only hear the forest crack.
My footprints disappear behind me.

I am right here but you would never know.
I am right here. You are never alone.

《冬诗四章》

I

天空以纷扬的彩屑
庆祝这季节的典仪

群山与林木隐没
只有低处风声粗砺

和林间里断裂的声音
足迹在身后逐一消逝

你永远不知 我就在此处
我就在此处 你永不孤独

II

Anyone driving a car is suddenly drunk.
The birds hide deep in the evergreens.

We have to seek out spaces of light
and follow them in order to get there.

Each little snowflake is a twirling ghost
slowly spinning down in the darkest night,

circling the candle lights in every house,
blown from the snow hats on the high mountains.

II

驾驶员都突然醉了
鸟儿全部躲进松林

在时间的缝隙里寻路
我们顺着光抵达终点

每片雪花都是旋转的幽魂
在最黑的夜里缓缓地飘落

在白雪皑皑的山岭上
家家都有环绕的烛光

III

Legions of snowflakes parachute to the ground.
They turn all the cars into white helmets.

Kids arch backwards, catching flakes with their tongues.
Beijing has turned into a big white ghost.

Snow has blanketed each of the Ring Roads,
slowed all the bicycles on the streets,

popped open all the people's umbrellas,
and has put boots on every pair of feet.

III

漫天的伞兵从天而降
将所有的车辆变作雪盔

孩子们伸出舌头，迎接雪花
北京一夜间成为巨大的幽灵

雪毯覆压每条环线道路
迟缓了街巷流转的车轮

撑开所有行人的伞骨
为每双脚踝套上靴筒

IV

The moonlight shines cold on the dead
bones scattered all over the old battlefield.

All the armor and the blood are long gone
but what happened here will always be told.

The screech owls will never stop moaning.
They are shaking in fading Mulberry trees.

The field mice squeal back to their holes
trying to hide from this permanent winter.

IV

月光冷冷的洒落在
古战场上的白骨

甲胄与血迹早已湮灭
但历史却在此地永驻

仓鸮在枯萎的桑树里颤抖
它们何时会停止无尽的呜咽

田鼠尖叫着逃回洞穴
躲避这永恒的冬天

Emperor Wu

None of us maidens will get married
until the Emperor's goat and buggy

have come through our village looking for love.
I hear he's coming from Fergana Valley.

I have a lute player in the background.
I let down my hair. I loosen my robe.

I hope Emperor Wu's goats are hungry.
I lay out bamboo and a pinch of salt.

《武帝》

我们这些姑娘谁也不嫁
除非武帝的山羊车驾

来我们村里寻访芳华
听说他正从大宛出发

背后有琴师轻拨丝弦
我散下发髻松开罗衫

摆好青竹与一撮盐巴
盼着武帝的山羊嘴馋

The Chosen One, Du Fu

The famine whispered into my aunt's ear
that she didn't have room for every child.

The child who sleeps in the southeast bedroom
is the child that hunger will keep alive.

My aunt took her son from the southeast room.
She tucked me in to sleep there for the night.

This is why I can always see the light.
I wish I had a chance to say good-bye.

《天选之子·杜甫》

饥荒在姑姑耳边喃喃低语：
你已无力抚养所有的孩子。

睡在东南厢房的那个，将被
饥饿赦免，成为天选之子。

姑姑把亲儿抱出东南厢房，
将我安顿在那张床上过夜。

于是我总能看到光。而我终身的
遗憾：那晚未与姑姑道别。

Lady Guogua's Spring Outing

We dress in the men's riding clothes.
We smile as we wave to the Palace Guard

and gallop into the forest. Some hide
the men's clothes under the trees to ride.

The rest decide to be men for a day.
Horses keep secrets. My *rugun* silk gown

flows with my horse's white tail and the clouds.
I return home with a gold *Han* headpiece.

《虢国夫人春游图》

我们换上男式骑装出发，
含笑挥别宫门前的禁卫，

策马驰入密林。有人
换上藏在树下的男装。

有人决意效仿男儿，跨上雄壮的
坐骑。我的襦裙丝裳翩跹，

与马尾白云相映成趣。
缓步归来，金箔汉服簪微颤。

Chang'an Dream

Our little boat is moving fairly smoothly
up the Wei River away from Chang'an.

Today is loud and bright and open wide,
but at the same time empty and quiet.

Our eyes alternate from river to shore.
Our minds are filled with our conversation.

We are too quiet to be heard in the noise.
We are too small to be seen from the sky.

《长安梦》

我们的小舟溯渭河而上
悄声无息地漂离出长安。

今日的日子明亮喧嚷，
旷远无边，空寂安宁。

我们的视线回荡在河岸与流水，
我们的心溢满未说完的对话。

我们的静默，喧闹中无人听闻，
我们的微小，苍穹下无处可见。

Wild Goose Pagoda

From high in the Wild Goose Pagoda
you see nothing but miles of open field.

Parades of millet with golden tassels wave
beside floating moats of green rice paddies.

The barn was that pile of bricks and broken roof.
The farmer wore a big conical hat.

His wife made it with her bare hands
to cover his face with shade every day.

《雁塔远眺》

从大雁塔顶端眺望
宽阔的田野无边无际

成片的小米垂下金色流苏
在绿油油的稻渠两边摇荡

粮仓在砖瓦堆与破屋顶下
如同农夫头上宽大的斗笠

那是他妻子亲手编织
为他日日遮挡烈日

Zhuangzi

I became a butterfly in my sleep.
I fluttered happy under the sunshine.

I flew in the clear skies, completely free.
I never felt so full of emptiness.

When I woke up I became a new me.
I wasn't sure which me I really was.

Am I a me with a new clarity
or that butterfly with a pair of wings?

《庄子》

梦里，我变成一只蝴蝶，
在阳光下，快乐地飞来飞去。

湛蓝的天空，从未如此清澈自由
这无边的空旷，也从未如此充盈。

醒来后，我不再是原来的我，
分不清哪一个才是真实——

是突然醒悟的我，
还是那有翅膀的蝴蝶？

Wine and Exile

The moon hangs low and wades on the river.
Empty wine jars clutter the wooden pier.
Li Bai leans back on his elbows, robes loose,
Du Fu stands with a cane, swaying back and forth.

Where is the hero of the eastern gate
you once said? I was drowning in taverns
scribbling hundreds of poems on my sleeves.
I woke up naked and my poems were gone!
My hair is white now, my ambitions undone—
the world's affairs are no longer worth mentioning.
Yet you still write of corrupt officials and starving soldiers...
Have another swig of wine and laugh instead!

In broken letters, I record these wandering years.
The people bleed while the ministers feast.
There is no one to mourn the bones on the road.
New ghosts wail, old ghosts weep.

《酒　　放逐》

月亮低垂，慢慢地走进河里
木码头上，堆满了空酒罐子
仰卧的李白，支着胳膊，衣带松散，
杜甫拄着手杖，醉的前俯后仰

你常提起的东门豪杰，他们在哪？
我每天在酒馆酩酊大醉，袖口里的诗
醒后全部无影无踪，身上也一丝不挂
如今白发苍苍，理想也泡了汤----
——世事不值一提。只有你
还在写贪官，饥饿的士兵
来吧，再喝一口，再笑一声！
我用破碎的词语，记下这动荡的年月。
百姓尸横遍野，大臣纸醉金迷
路边的尸骨，无人收殓
新鬼哭号，旧鬼呜咽

今晚醉得不省人事，谁能扶起这个王朝？
河里的星星，是光的宝石
文字能保存人类的思想，
却无法填饱一个人的肚子？

We're too drunk to save the empire tonight.
The stars in the river are jewels of light.
Words may preserve a man's thoughts,
but can they fill a single empty belly?
My thatched roof was torn by autumn winds—
what use is fame when children shiver?
The times are hard—in this generation, we are useless.
Yet here we sit, two old fools by the water
watching the moon as if it were ours to keep.
Let this wine be our momentary monument.
The universe is but an inn for all creatures.
Time is merely a passing traveler.
You can turn a gallon of wine into a hundred poems.
The characters you write are bare tree shadows.

Grasp this pleasure, who knows if we'll be
alive tomorrow to share another jar of wine.
All my life I've been chasing after something,
the road ahead is running out of time.
Tonight I found that something here with you.
When will we drink by the parted fence again?

秋风撕烂我的茅屋顶——
孩子冻得发抖时，名声有个屁用
这年头—我们这代人算是 废了
可我们还坐在河边，两个老傻瓜
盯着月亮 像盯着自己的存款

让这杯酒来祭奠我们的临时墓碑
天地是万物的客栈　　光阴只是过客
你能把酒 变成一百首诗
写出的词语，全是破碎的星辰
抓紧这快乐的时光吧， 谁知道
明天还能不能 一起喝酒
我一辈子都在追寻莫名的目标
而前面的路，漫长的让人绝望。
今晚总算找到你了。
何时再隔着篱笆饮酒?

Chanzu

Your feet are wrapped in long strips of tight cloth.
In ten years they become golden lilies.

You will never run again. You will walk
slow on your heels for the rest of your life.

The pain is gone after you stop growing.
You learn the lotus steps of swift lightness.

When you marry you will bring a fine price.
You will be followed by the peasant masses.

《缠足》

长长的布条缠住你的双脚
直到十年后裹出一对金莲。

从次你再也不能奔跑，只能
踩着脚跟，缓步走过你的余生。

剧烈的疼痛伴随着你长大
直到你学会莲步，轻如点水。

出嫁时，你的金莲将卖个好价钱
而民间的姑娘们都会争相效仿。

Lin Zexu

Ashen faces, weak breath, black teeth, and hollow,
our soldiers can no longer stand to fight.

I've had all the pipes smashed to pieces,
the opium poured out into open pools.

We knead it with our feet into a stew
then cover it with lime and salt for days.

We open up the gate and let it flow
to sea. We pray for fish that die today.

《林则徐》

面如死灰，气息奄奄，齿黑颊凹，
将士们吸毒成瘾，早已无力再战。

我命人将烟管尽数捣毁，
把成桶的鸦片抛入水塘。

士兵们赤足跳入，把毒品踩成泥浆，
然后加厚厚的石灰和盐，淹没数日。

最后开闸泄流，让祸水直入大海。
惟愿今日毙命之鱼，魂得安息。

Off the Fourth Ring Road
四环之外

Before Stephon Marbury or Yao Ming

Back when Wanfujing still had People's Hotels
someone stole your purse when you weren't looking.

This was long before Stephon Marbury and Yao Ming
hovered on big screens overlooking the street.

You lost all your money and passport.
The US embassy said shame on you.

You should be more careful. There is nothing
we can do to help you but write it down.

《斯蒂芬·马布里与姚明之前的年代》

那时，王府井还保留着人民旅馆的气息
那时，有人趁你不注意夹走了你的钱包

那时，斯蒂芬·马布里与姚明
还未浮上街头街角的屏幕

那时，你丢了全部现金和护照
美国大使馆说：我真替你害臊

领事训斥：是你自己粗心大意
我们除了记录，实在鞭长莫及

THE WAY

Your bag happened to land in the right basket.
The thief took your money and he threw

your purse into a sea of bicycles.
When the bike's owner returned to her bike

she found the purse and the hotel's card inside.
She biked all the way back to Beijing.

She returned your purse back at the hotel.
She rode away without leaving her name.

《道》

小偷掏空钱后，顺手把皮夹
抛入自行车的海洋

你的包落进她的车筐
当车主回到她的车子

发现里面的皮夹和酒店卡片
便骑车穿过整个城市

将失物交给酒店前台
然后蹬车离去，不留姓名

Wedding Dress

Kelly went over to the Silk District
to buy some silk for her wedding gown.

She could smell and feel centuries of trade.
The woman back in Colorado who sewed

her clothes when she was a kid had one last run.
The Chinese saleswoman smiled at the news

and returned with glowing rolls of red fabric.
Kelly said 'white please' and got a frown.

《婚纱》

凯莉去了趟丝绸市场
想买些料子做婚纱

闻着几千年流传下来的交易
她想起小时候在科罗拉多州那个最后

一次为她量衣的裁缝。中国女店员
喜开颜笑地捧出红彤彤的绸缎卷

“凯莉说 “我只要白色的”
她眉头紧凑，脸色大变

A Chinese Husband

I can squint at the Chinese characters
on the busy street signs all day long

and nine out of ten times I take a right
that should be a left, a left that should be a right.

I was so impressed to see Kelly speak
Chinese and be right when she said go right.

Kelly's Chinese friends said her Chinese would be
better if she had a Chinese husband.

《中国丈夫》

我可以整天眯着眼，
琢磨街牌上缭花眼乱的汉字。

十次有九次，该右转时我左转，
该左转时我右转。

我着实佩服凯莉的中文，
她说“右拐”，还真说对了。

凯莉的中国朋友说，
找个中国丈夫，她的中文会更好。

September 11

I left you in Beijing on September 8th,
I had to paint the walls at our new place.

A few days later the planes hit New York.
One of the planes lost Pete, Sue, and their baby.

We found out that your brother was okay.
Our Chinese friends found you a place to stay—

with VPN and TV. We got you home.
To the US by plane. To Boston by train.

《911》

9月8日我把你留在北京
我先回去粉刷新家的墙壁

几天后飞机突袭纽约。坠毁的那一架
载着皮特、苏和他们的孩子

得知你弟弟安然无恙
中国朋友为你找了个房间——

配有VPN和电视。我们终于接你回家
先乘航班回美利坚，然后转火车到波士顿

Pound

I first read a version of Cathay
at the Trident in 1986

about a month after the Celtics
won their 16th championship.

I saw the black and white New Directions
book in the window after the parade.

My hair was still cut quite straight back then.
The book fit right in my green tweed pocket.

《庞德》

1986年，我在三城
第一次看到《华夏集》。

那天，凯尔特人球队
刚夺下第十六个冠军。

游行结束，突然见到橱窗里那本
黑白封面的书，《新方向》出版。

那时我的头发，剪得齐齐整整
《华夏集》正好塞进我的绿花呢口袋。

Happy Birthday

I.

I think the worst birthday I ever had
was flying to Beijing with two young kids

in Economy Class before the iPad.
The party didn't end when we landed.

Instead of going straight to bed after
screaming for twelve hours on the flight,

both kids thought they made it home.
They were wide awake and ready to play.

《生日快乐》

一

我想最糟的一次生日
是带俩娃飞北京经济舱

那会儿还没iPad
飞机降落，派对还在继续

飞机上尖叫了十二个钟头
孩子们不但不困

反而以为到家了
两眼放光，要接着玩

II

My kids were waking everyone up—
singing songs and shouting at the hotel.

Daddy, Daddy why don't you want to play with me?
I said it was the middle of the night.

They didn't understand so I gave up
and took them on an elevator ride.

My kids made the cooks in the kitchen happy.
We left wearing Chef's hats and watermelon.

二

俩娃在酒店又唱又跳
把所有人全部闹醒——

爸爸爸爸为啥不陪我玩？
我说现在是半夜呀

他们听不懂， 我只好投降
带他们坐电梯，上下兜风

厨房师傅被娃娃逗得直乐
临走塞给他们厨师帽和西瓜

Beijing Bike

I

I bought my yellow bike from this guy far out
on the Fifth Ring Road for one hundred kuài.

Squatting like a catcher on the sidewalk.
Smoking cigarettes in a white tank top.

Fixing flats, pumping tires, selling bikes.
He grew up with his dad doing this in Chengdu.

He goes home to celebrate the New Year.
I rode the bike all year and sold it back to him.

《北京单车》

I

在五环外 我从一个家伙那儿
买了这辆黄色单车， 一百元

他蹲在人行道上，像个捕快
身穿白色背心， 抽着烟头

补胎 打气 卖二手车
在成都 他从小就跟父亲干

每年春节他回趟老家过年
我骑了一整年 又把车卖回给他

II

I put a banana seat on my bike
so I could take my son to school each day.

He thought he was floating in a parade
and would wave to everyone as we rode by.

Most of them waved back with a happy smile.
Not the day his ankle got caught in the spokes

on our way back home from the grocery store.
The bike seized. They couldn't stop screaming.

II

我给单车装了香蕉座
每天骑着送儿子上学

他觉得自己在游行车里漂浮
一路上对每个人挥手致意

人人都微笑着挥手招呼
那天从杂货店回家

他的脚踝被卡进链条
车子停下，西奥还是尖叫不止

Fourth Ring Road, 2010

There are traffic lights now,
the drivers act like
they are always green.

A *Tsinghua* student
in purple
slowly pumps
his heavy steel bicycle
across Zhongguancun East
and Shaungqing Road—

like a lone duck
fluttering between
moving ocean liners
in Hong Kong harbor.

The sky is blue
way up above us
and August is hot,
he sweats right through.

《四环路上，2010》

如今有了红绿灯
司机们却仿佛
只看得见绿色。

一个清华学子，身着紫衫
蹬着沉重的钢架车
缓缓穿过
中关村东与双清路交汇处——

像只孤零零的鸭子
扑棱着翅膀
穿梭香港
远洋巨轮的间隙。

我们头顶，天空湛蓝
燥热的八月
湿透他的衣衫。

雾霾与微尘
模糊了街道
也模糊了他的眼镜。

Smog and particulates
fog up the street
and his glasses.

Riding side-saddle
with him
is his girlfriend.

She holds an umbrella,
big sunglasses,
cool in a pale pink dress

with navy azaleas
and a long serpent
sticking out its tongue

My son waves to her
from the back of my bike.

She smiles back
through her doctor's mask.

后座侧坐着
是他的姑娘。

撑着阳伞
戴着大墨镜
浅粉的长裙，沁着凉意

裙摆上海蓝色的杜鹃
窜出蟒蛇，　吐着信子

我儿子从自行车后座
朝她挥手

她透过医生的口罩
对我们微笑。

Chinese Lessons

I spent one hundred renminbi each week
paying a tutor to teach me Chinese.

I would try to practice every night
at dinner in the cafeteria.

My five year-old would get so excited
when the waiter would bring out a live fish.

But he would plead with me to not speak Chinese.
'They'll know we are foreigners!' he'd say.

《中文课》

每周我花一百块，
请老师辅导中文。

每天食堂开晚饭，
我总是努力练习。

五岁的儿子看见活鱼端上桌，
就会开心得活蹦乱跳。

然后拽着我的袖口哀求：
别说中文了，好嘛——
你一开口，他们就知道我们是老外.

To Market, To Market

Back in Boston the town was building
a new school across the street. Theo would watch

the big yellow trucks and cranes with amazement.
In Beijing he loves to go to market.

What lychee! What peaches and penumbras!
By far the flailing fish tank was the best.

The monger sticks his bare hands in the tank.
She grabs a fish and slaps him still on the bar.

《赶集，赶集》

回到波士顿，街对面正在建新校。
儿子西奥总会惊奇地观望

那些黄色的大卡车和起重机。
在北京，他最爱的还是赶集。

多么甜美的水桃荔枝！多么奇妙的光影！
但最有趣的还数那个水花四溅的鱼缸——

鱼贩赤手伸进缸里，捞起一条鱼，
“啪”地一声，摔在案板上。

Dear Ming

Dear Ming. I am now back in Beijing.
Please send me an email with your address

in Mandarin characters. I will hand
it to my driver, close my eyes, and pray!

Please also include your cell phone number.
You told me the new cab drivers come in

from the countryside looking for a new life
but can't read. I may need to call for help.

《亲爱的敏》

亲爱的敏，我回北京啦。
请把你的地址发给我。

要带中文的，我可以交给
出租车司机，闭上眼，祈祷！

请附上你的电话号码。
你曾说过北京有很多来自

乡村的农民讨新生活，但他们
不识字。我可能需要打电话求助。

Tsinghua Daswei

All I had to say was 'Tsinghua Daswei,'
or 'let's go to Tsinghua University.'

Then the driver would say something. 'Dongmen'
is what I was supposed to say in response—

short for 'please drop me off at the East Gate.'
None of the drivers knew what I was saying.

I would call my wife and hand the driver my phone.
He'd look back and say oh 'Tsinghua Daswei!'

《清华打穗》

我只需说一声"清华大穗"，
或"咱们去 "Tsinghua University"。

司机便会明白，然后我加一句"东门"
那是"请让我在东门下"的简称——

可惜没有一个司机听明白我在说什么。
我只好打电话给太太，将手机递到前面。

司机回头一看，恍然大悟：
"哦——清华大'学'啊！"

The China Daily is Talking to Me

The China Daily is talking to me
anywhere in the world in English--

even right here in downtown Beijing.
I buy a paper version for a few kuài

after I drop my son off at his school.
I read about the sun outside Beijing.

I read about the NBA back home.
But something seems to be missing.

《中国日报》在对我说话

无论我走到世界的任何角落——
《中国日报》都用英语，和我说话

甚至在北京城的中心。
送完儿子上学，我总是花几块钱

买份报纸，浏览那些
关于北京城外阳光的报道

还有故乡NBA的新闻。
看了半天，心里总觉得缺了点什么。

VPN

I read Maisy the Mouse to Estelle.
I kept her in touch with Nana on Skype.

I read the FT and the New York Times.
I would secretly stream Bloomberg TV.

After dropping Theo off at his school
I buy a China Daily for two kuài.

By the East Gate near Tsinghua University,
I learn how to read between the lines.

《翻墙纪事》

给艾丝黛尔念小鼠波波的故事，
用Skype让她和奶奶视频相见。

读金融时报与纽约时报的晨讯，
偷连彭博电视的财经新闻。

一大早送西奥去学校，然后
买一份两块钱的《中国日报》。

在清华东门外的长椅上，
细品字里行间的深意。

Oppen at the Expo

You pulled my hair out riding on my shoulders.
Arms around my head, a child queen

on an elephant tiptoeing heavy
across the world at the Shanghai Expo.

You dug your fingers and fists in my scalp
so hard, if it wasn't you I'd have screamed.

I was so happy you could see all this,
I just winced and gripped both your ankles tight.

《奥本在博览会》

你揪着我的头发，骑在我的肩头
双臂环抱我的头顶，像个小女王

骑着大象，游览世界博览会
踮着脚尖，沉重地走过上海。

你的手指和拳头抠进我头皮，
那么用力，换别人我早大声喊疼。

可我想让你看清这一切，
便默默地攥紧你的脚踝。

Just Like Home

Theo and Estelle ran under the spring
Maple Trees at Xiangshan Park.

Each green seed is two little wings kissing
each other with sticky noses on their faces.

They swarmed in little clouds of wind, hundreds
of spinning green helicopters just like home.

Just like home my kids chase them under the sky.
Just like home my kids stick them on their noses.

《回家》

春天到了，香撒公园的枫林下，
西奥和埃斯特奔跑跳跃。

每颗青翠的种子都带着翅膀
贴在鼻尖，亲吻粘稠的脸庞。

它们成群地盘旋，在风中组成片片绿色云彩
千百架旋转的直升机——带我们飞回老家。

如同老家的天空，孩子们追逐带有翅膀的枫叶
如同老家的天空，孩子们将绿色种子贴上鼻尖。

Looking for the Way

All I did was pluck a cherry blossom
and eat it pretending it was ice cream.

Then other thoughts made me drift away.
I was thinking of ten thousand things.

I didn't see you make that funny face—
a response to mine in the first place.

Was that the way I was supposed to go?
Can I be in both spaces at the same time?

《寻道》

我摘下一朵樱花
当作冰淇淋咽下

千头万绪载着我漂流
我的心也漂着千头万绪

没看见你做的鬼脸——
那原本是对我的回应

难道那就是该走的路？
我怎样才能同时身处两地？

Well Rounded

All the time we were living in Beijing
I couldn't get enough of the food.

I loved to order the Squirrel Fish.
First it would come flapping in a black bag

and make Theo jump up and down laughing.
It came back orange, filleted, fried, sweet, and sour

with pork dumplings, green beans, watermelon.
I returned to Boston quite well rounded.

《圆满》

在北京居住的那些日子
我总也吃不够京城的美味

尤爱点那道松鼠鳜鱼
裹着黑袋端上桌时扑棱作响

逗得西奥蹦跳着笑个不停
再上桌时，起鳞油炸 金黄透亮 甜酸适口

佐以猪肉饺子 清炒豆角 冰镇西瓜
归返波士顿时，我早已体态丰盈

The Morning Darkness

It is close to impossible to see
through clouds of pollution in front of me.

I don't feel so free when I'm driving here.
Everyone has to be at work by nine.

If you drove today you are late again.
There is just one Ring Road after another.

Even the subways are running behind.
Police wear the masks, not the thieves.

《晨昏》

视线几乎穿不透
眼前厚重的雾霾

路上行驶, 感受不到自由
人人都需九点前到岗

今日驾车，注定再次迟到
环线道路层层嵌套，连绵不绝

就连地铁也延误了
小偷，不，是警察戴上了口罩

TRANSLATION

Our daughter was only one and a half
when we lived in Beijing. She didn't

have very much to say. She didn't like
the heat and we wonder about the food.

She covered her face with canned spaghetti
the only time we bought it. Years later

when we shared we were moving to Washington
she replied, 'do they speak English down there?'

《翻译》

住北京时，咱闺女才一岁半
整天窝在家里，很少说话

天热，老是吃不下饭，唯一的一次
为她买了罐意大利通心粉，她抹得满脸通红

多年后 我们要搬回华盛顿
她仰头问：“那儿的人说英文么？”

AliPay Annals
支付宝账单

Before another Flight

The sky is as gray as an oyster shell.
The Charles echoes looking frozen solid.

The Sycamore trees have lost all their leaves.
They branch out like the long prickly fingers

of all the old Brahmins on Bay State Road.
The rats are now much easier to see.

The Bald Eagle swoops down for a feast.
In front of my window, she spreads her wings.

《又一次起飞》

天是牡蛎的灰
回声把查尔斯河凝成冰道

脱光了叶子的悬铃木，多刺的枝桠
如同海湾路上那些爆燥的婆罗门

老鼠招摇过街
白头鹰俯冲捕食

划过我的窗前
撑起一座天空

Beijing Spring

All the trees and flowers are crying
with spring happiness. Seeds and petals fly

from their eyes, flutter in the sky,
then sprinkle the earth as confetti.

Cardinals and Robins are back to get fat.
They bury their beaks in the seeds to feast—

so much so not much grows around here—
except for the eggs in the nests of birds.

《北京之春》

万木与百花携着春日的
欢喜哭泣。种子与花瓣

飞出视线， 在蓝天下飞舞
然后化为彩屑， 遍洒大地

红衣凤头与知更鸟早已归来
长喙深入花蕾，尽情饱餐

繁忙的林间，此处却草木稀疏——
唯有春光在巢中等待破壳

Morris Graves in the Summer Palace

In far corners of the Summer Palace
near the fog rolling over the muddy pools

is a little-known bird of the inner eye
that makes the water clear to see through.

A bird maddened by the length of winter,
loud in the fog like a wounded raven.

Unfolding with a permanence of change,
a place of value in a world of facts.

《颐和园——追忆莫里斯·格雷夫斯》

颐和园深处
薄雾滚过泥潭的角落

那里有鲜为人知的小鸟
将水面拭得澄明如镜

被漫长冬季逼疯的鸟儿
如受伤的乌鸦在雾里嘶叫

这无常的世界
仍有让人流连忘返的栖所

Asleep at Sea

Wooden ships sound like old rocking chairs
when the wind or waves roll to the shore.

The wet ropes tapping their metal masts
are natural wind chimes in the harbor night.

The real captain's bells slowly sound off.
Not loud enough to wake anyone up.

All a slow chorus of low xylophones,
just calm enough to put us all to sleep.

《海上小夜曲》

风推着浪花，涌入港口
木船嘎嘎吱吱，如同老旧的摇椅

湿透的缆绳轻叩金属桅杆
那是港夜天然的风铃

船长的铃铛缓缓地摇摆
却唤不醒任何人的梦境

铃声带我们沉入睡眠
随着木琴般的低音合唱

Misty

Our backs were bent over like question marks.
Our lives were measured in bags of rice.

We wore our own clothes and conical hats.
We carted to market on makeshift bikes.

We now stand up as exclamation points.
We build big factories and shadow banks

hedged by skyscrapers and hovering cranes.
The sky's new soot is darker than the sea.

《雾》

我们的脊梁曾被弯压成问号
我们的生命曾以米袋子衡量

穿着自织的粗布　戴着自编的斗笠
我们推着改装的板车　一步步迈向市场

如今我们以惊叹号的姿态站立
建起巨型工厂与影子银行体系

塔吊在摩天楼群穿梭自如
天空里的烟尘比海水还深

Tempest after Kenneth Rexroth

Neither history or nature is moral.
Matter rebels and energy escapes.

Our dreams are interrupted by the clowns
who use matter to destroy our village life.

We will have to overcome them once again:
with love and the forgiveness of evil,

among the timeless unities of care,
on stage for the unreality of time.

《肯尼斯.雷克斯罗特的风暴》

历史与自然没有道德的尺度
物质可以叛变 能量也会逃逸

小丑以物质毁灭我们的村子
我们的美梦因此半途而废

我们将再次超越他们:
以爱来宽恕恶的黑暗

让无限的大爱 永远
立于虚妄时间的舞台上

Festival of Kites

It is Saturday. Please take my granddaughter
to the Temple of Heaven to fly a kite.

The blue sky is clear and the wind is strong.
Let her join the parade up in the skies.

I know that all the other mother's girls
are tied to their desks studying for the test.

Remember that Du Fu failed his exams.
Now he flies even higher than the kites.

《风筝节》

今天星期六 请带我的孙女
去天坛放风筝吧

明亮的蓝天，风呼呼地刮
让孩子也加入空中的游行

我知道别人家的女儿
正伏在桌前应付考试

你可知杜甫也曾经落第
如今他飞得比风筝更高更远

Tiantan Gongyuan

No longer popular
with the sons of heaven
who would come here
to seek atonement
or to offer ceremonial rites
in return for a generous yield,
the Temple of Heaven
is now an island for kites.

Once forbidden to all
but the son himself,
the sacred marble path
that connects each temple
serves as the runway
for anyone who can fly.

At daybreak parades of men,
women, and children
look like they are being
chased by laughing dragons
as they run for cover toward the
Hall of Prayer for Good Harvest.

《天坛公园》

不再得宠的天子
会来此处　祈求宽恕
或举行祭典
祈祷丰年
而如今的天坛
成了风筝的岛屿
曾经是天子独行的
大理石圣道

通往每一座殿宇
如今化作跑道
服务所有飞风筝的人
破晓时分
男女老少列队而行
仿佛被欢笑的龙

追逐着
奔向祈年殿躲避
一个刹那
一个回首
龙突然化为纸　停驻 盘旋
然后天使般乘风而起

But at the right moment,
with one sharp glance
over the shoulder, the dragons
turn into paper, halt, hover,
then angelically ascend to the wind
as their string leashes spin
through the fingers of their masters.

The kites soon look
like little black worms
as their fliers fish for more wind
in the sky's cloudy pools.

线绳
在主人指间飞转
风筝很快变成
丁丁点点的黑虫
放飞的人们
在云池里 垂钓更多的风

A Letter

Mosquitos swarm in cursive and sting you
each time you stick your toe in the river.

It's always ice cold regardless of the weather.
Moonlight picks out the cotton in the fields

as constellations of stars on the earth.
Clouds of darkness form in your mental sky.

Carry those burdens high to the mountaintop
and leave them behind up there forever.

《信》

每当你赤足探进河水
成群的蚊子狂草般扑来

一年四季　这里总是一片沁寒
棉花地里 月光在细细挑拣

星群坠落 碎成遍地光点
浓云的暗影 聚在你心头

将沉重的心思背上山
让它们永远留在峰顶

Second Ring Road

You only talk in your kitchen. He lies
in her lap under a Tapa Cloth Tree.

That doesn't mean they don't have jobs.
They are just falling in love in the shade.

Fried pork jiaozi lie like fish on their sides.
Rice steams clouds of white silky ways.

You don't idle under a Tapa Cloth tree.
You close the door and start singing to me.

《二环路》

你只在厨房里说话
他只愿在榕树底下　躺在她的膝边

这不代表他们不肯工作
他们相爱 在树荫下微凉

煎饺像鱼 并排侧卧
米饭蒸腾　升起银河般的云朵

你如今　不再去榕树下闲坐
只是关上门　对我歌唱

I don't see anything to believe in

I don't see anything to believe in
except the world right in front of me.

The Chinese Paddlefish has disappeared.
Wild Yaks shake the earth when they fall to death.

There's nothing worse than burying a friend.
Orange leaves curl into fists of red dust.

Mountains, flowers, water and the free sky.
People, trees, animals and just living.

《我不再相信》

除了我眼前的世界
我不再相信

中华鲟早已绝迹
野牦牛倒地的声音　震撼地球

最悲痛欲绝的时刻　莫如埋葬好友
卷曲的秋叶　握紧团团红尘

山麓，花朵，流水，浮云
人群，树林，野兽，依旧活着

Coffin Home

I have one of the most expensive flats
in Hong Kong at 500 pounds per square foot.

For my sleeping matt, my minifridge, and me.
My little place is twenty square feet.

I share a toilet and a shower stall
with just twenty other people in this room.

I sit up quick to see what happened
and smack my head at the top of my cage.

《棺房》

这是我在香港租下的豪宅
每平方尺 活生生的五千港币

整整二十平方尺的豪屋
刚好摆下床垫冰箱和我的身体

还有二十人共用的厕浴
也挤在这间豪宅

我坐起来看出了什么事
砰的一声 额头撞上笼顶

Attack of the Mongols, 2024

The sands of Mongolia have blown
all the way to Beijing and seized the day.

The sky is dark but we are wearing shades
to protect our eyes from sharp sand flying.

Everyone wears mask on the streets again.
There are no flights in or out of the sky.

The government calls it a holiday.
The best thing to do is just stay inside.

《蒙古袭击·二〇二四》

蒙古的黄沙卷入北京
一口气劫走了白昼

天色昏沉 我们戴上墨镜
躲闪那些飞翔的利刃

街面上人们又戴上口罩
航班在天空里绝了踪迹

政府宣布今天放晴假
最好的对策是闭门不出

April 2025

Typhoon-like gales shut down Beijing today.
The windows on the skyscrapers are shaking.

The trees in the parks bend like question marks.
Umbrellas escape to the skies like wild kites.

Air planes wobble in like drunken cranes.
The government shuts down all the flights.

Passengers vomit as they touch the ground,
even Lin. All the luggage is left behind.

《四月2025》

台风般的狂风让北京停摆
摩天楼的窗格在气流中震颤

公园里的树弯成无数问号
伞群挣脱人手 化作野风筝远去

航班像醉鹤在云端踉跄
政府掐灭了所有航线的信号灯

触地时 小林和所有的乘客都捧着纸袋
狂呕　只有行李在转盘上孤独地盘旋

Songs for Kelly

I

I am twelve hours ahead in Beijing.
6 pm and just back to my room.

Rexroth is standing beside you in bed
about now, then he jumps in to cuddle.

You put your coffee on and give him his pill,
put on his leash, and take him up the hill.

Boston is hard to see through the spring trees.
Estelle wakes up by the time you are back.

《给凯莉的歌》

I

北京时间 比你那儿早十二个小时
傍晚六点 我才回房歇息

此刻雷克斯罗特正趴在你的床畔
等着跳入被窝，与你依偎

你煮上咖啡 哄他吞下药粒
系好牵绳 带他漫步上山坡

春树繁茂 遮住波士顿倩影
回家时 埃斯特尔刚好醒来

II

The great steel cranes are finally sitting still
over Beijing. The dust they made has settled.

The night sky over the city is now all clear.
Little lights on the cranes echo the stars.

You see the Autumn moon from your hotel room.
The same full moon I saw back here at home,

last night when our kids were in a deep sleep,
when I was 'wakeful while the long night goes.'

II

钢铁的巨臂终于歇息
北京的上空，尘埃也已落地

城市的夜空，澄明安宁
塔上的灯光与星辰相映

从酒店的窗口凝望秋月
满满的月光，牵引家乡的圆盈

昨夜在孩子们的梦乡里
我独自 倾听长夜的流逝

III

Your mother is back in Boston with the kids.
We are alone in Beijing for a week.

We go out for duck in the evening.
We walk back holding hands through Wanfujing.

Each day you have to run to your meetings.
I go to mine in the other direction.

We do nothing but sleep for the first few nights.
Tonight we are up late making love.

III

母亲带着孩子回了波士顿
留下你我独守北京的光阴

晚上我们出门去吃烤鸭
然后沿着王府井牵手回家

白天你赶赴城南的会议
我穿行城北去我的会场

头几夜我们只顾相拥而眠
今夜，我们缠绵直至星沉

IV

The first time we walked down Wanfujing
you could still see the Western Hills from the street.

There were only Peoples stores selling Mao's
little red books, keychains, and Forbidden Cities.

The talk of the town was the McDonald's
and its line around Chang 'an into the hutongs.

Now Stephon Marbury hovers over us
brighter at night than under the sun today.

IV

第一次我们在王府井漫步
从大街上 还望得见西山

只有人民商店摆着毛主席的
红宝书 钥匙扣 还有故宫模型

满城都在议论新开张的麦当劳
队伍从长安街蜿蜒穿进胡同

如今斯蒂芬·马布里横跨夜空
比中午的太阳更加灼热耀眼

Who are We Worried About?

When we said we're going back to China
we were told to bring freshly wiped computers

and cellphones. 'Leave all your devices home.
Delete everything before you come back.'

The devices they issued us packed light
and got through on the Chinese side just fine—

but they worked like typewriters in the fifties,
like old payphones where all your dimes get stuck.

《我们担忧什么》

去中国前　他们千叮万嘱：
彻底清除所有的电脑、手机。

“回美国前，务必删除所有的文件
任何电子设备都不能带回家.”

配给我们的电脑轻飘而单薄
过中国海关倒是畅通无阻——

用起来却像五十年代的打字机
像投币电话被硬币卡住了脖子

The State is Destroyed. The Country Remains.

—Du Fu

The state is destroyed. The country remains.
Cherry trees hold down their pink clouds of spring.

The White Mountains let go of their snow,
it flows from the peaks through creeks and rivers.

Black bear and deer drink from the fresh cold lakes.
Farmers build furrow dikes for their crops.

The fires and floods have been wild for three months now.
As we to the trees, the trees to rocks and hills.

国破山河在—杜甫

国虽破了，山河仍然依旧
樱花树拉缀着粉红的春天。

冰川顶上 解冻的积雪
顺着山麓，奔流不息。

黑熊与麋鹿啜饮清冷的湖水。
农人为秋收，筑起条条沟垄。

整整三个月，水火交织
我们依偎树木，如同树木依偎石头与山崖。

THERE IS NO CLASS WHEN YOU LOSE A WAR

There is no class when you lose a war.
Rich and poor are both running for the hills.

Our children scream with fear, bite us with hunger.
Perfumed faces, now dried out old maps.

Servants hide the Noble as their servants.
Neither can gather their family's bones.

To the mountains and rivers without end.
No cart tracks to follow. Jumble of stones.

《战败后人人平等》

战败后的日子 人人平等
富人穷人 一齐逃往山里

孩子们在恐惧中尖叫 饿得张口咬人
涂脂抹粉的脸庞 干涸成破旧的地图

贵族装扮成仆从的仆人
可无人能带回亲人的骸骨

绵延的山川 从此不再有
车马痕迹 只有乱石嶙峋

Kevin P. Gallagher is a poet, publisher, and political economist living in Greater Boston, USA. He has published nine books of poems. His recent works are *And Yet it Moves* (Mad Hat, 2023), *The Wild Goose* (Loom Press, 2022), *Radio Plays* (Dos Madres, 2019), and *LOOM* (MadHat, 2016). Gallagher edits *spoKe*, a Boston-based annual of poetry and poetics. He works as a professor of global development policy at Boston University.

凯文·P·加拉格尔是一位身居美国大波士顿地区的诗人、出版人和政治经济学家。他已出版九部诗集，近年作品包括《然而它仍在转动》（MadHat出版社，2023年）、《野鹅》（Loom出版社，2022年）、《广播剧》（Dos Madres出版社，2019年）及《织机》（MadHat出版社，2016年）。加拉格尔主编波士顿诗歌与诗学年刊《spoKe》，同时担任波士顿大学全球发展政策学教授。

Ping Wang published 15 books of poetry & prose, including *The River within* (MadHat 2023), *My Name Is Immigrant (Hanging Loose 2021), Life of Miracles along Yangtze and Mississippi* (Georgia U, 2018), *Aching for Beauty* (Anchorage 2001). Her work was featured in NYT, PBS, BBC, Moth and others. She's recipient of NEA, Bush, Lannan, McKnight Fellowships, AWP Book Award and many others. She's founder/director of Kinship of Rivers project, Poetry Professor Emerita, Macalester College.

https://madhat-press.com/products/the-river-within-by-wang-ping

www.wangping.com

www.kinshipofrivers.org

王屏，祖籍威海，80届北大西语系，1985去纽约州大学攻读比较文学博士，出版15部诗歌及小时，包括《心中的河流》（MadHat出版社2023年）、《我的名字叫移民》（Hanging Loose出版社2021年）、《扬子江与密西西比河畔的奇迹人生》（佐治亚大学出版社2018年）、《为美而痛：三寸金莲》（安克雷奇出版社2001年）。《纽约时报》、美国公共电视网、英国广播公司、《飞蛾》故事会等知名媒体曾专题报道。她荣获美国国家艺术基金会、布什基金会、兰南基金会、麦肯奈特基金会等机构颁发的艺术奖项，AWP图书奖等诸多荣誉，马卡莱斯特学院终身教授，荣休诗歌教授，现任"河流的亲缘"公益项目创始人兼总监。

www.ingramcontent.com/pod-product-compliance
Lightning Source LLC
Chambersburg PA
CBHW021324060726
47591CB00006B/1855
9781969900129